Heartbeats

Poems for Christian Prayer, Praise and Biblical Reflection

ISBN-13: 978-1-7377620-6-5
ISBN-10: 1-7377620-6-4

First printing, June 2023

Cover design by ThomasMax

Published by:

ThomasMax Publishing
P.O. Box 250054
Atlanta, GA 30325
www.thomasmax.com

Heartbeats

Poems for Christian Prayer, Praise and Biblical Reflection

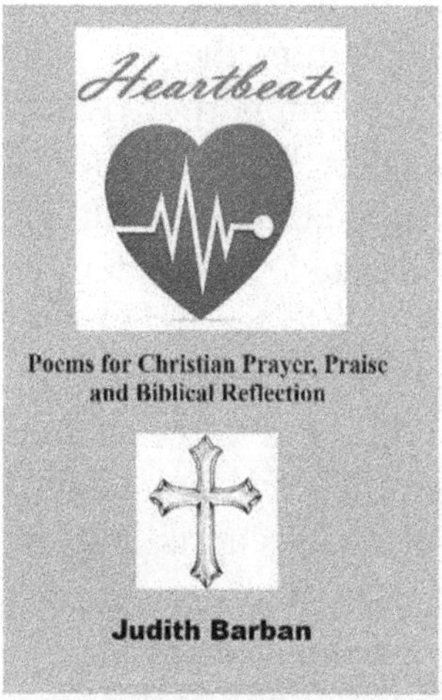

Poetry by

Judith Barban

ThomasMax

Your Publisher
For The 21st Century

Author's Preface

These poems were written over a period of about ten years, but they reflect a lifetime of agony and ecstasy. My journey with Jesus has not been a smooth one, but I can honestly say it has not been a boring one. As a young teen I accepted Christ as my Savior and spent the next few years filled with the joy of the Lord and living in a loving, Christian family environment. As I entered life on my own I began a rollercoaster ride that has not ended. I have known pain, sorrow, great disappointment, but also extreme joy—often in rapid succession. Just to give you an example, I was married at age nineteen to a popular evangelist. I was not in love, but I was overjoyed to think that I was in the center of God's will. I could serve not only as a supportive wife to a minister, but also organist/pianist at his crusades. Within a short time I came to the awful realization that he was a charlatan, a drug addict, a thief, and a homosexual pedophile. He made two attempts on my life: one with poison, one with a Colt 45. With the help of my mother, good doctors, and God's mercy I managed to escape.

I was awarded a Fulbright grant to France during the "beatnik" era. I joined in the spirit of the times, reading Camus, Sartre, and Simone de Beauvoir while dressed in black capris and black turtleneck, smoking unfiltered Gauloises cigarettes. Back home I became a "flower child" in a long, loose dress, handing out wildflowers on street corners and playing and singing folk songs on the guitar. Bob Dylan and Arlo Guthrie were my heroes. The times were indeed a-changing and before I knew it I was a full-fledged pot-smoking week-end "hippie." My life spiraled out of control and deeper into sin, yet all the while I worked hard at my college teaching job and was one of the most popular professors. I even managed to complete a PhD in Medieval French Language and Literature. I never stopped believing in God. I never stopped praying. But I wasn't living a Christian life.

Finally in 1978 I couldn't tolerate my shameful lifestyle, so I asked God for forgiveness and would He please take over. It wasn't long until I met the love of my life, an international concert pianist and artist-in-residence at a college in a neighboring state. This time I *was* in love—over the moon in love! We have been married 44 years now. But the agony and ecstasy has continued. Lows and highs have been the norm. Health issues, career issues, jealousy that turned friends into spiteful enemies, and huge disappointments. At one point a confluence of traumatic events left me almost totally light-sensitive and dealing with PTSD. I spent several months confined to a semi-dark room. With the help of my husband, a Pentecostal preacher's wife, a pianist friend, a holistic massage therapist, a wonderful chiropractor, and the right medication, I slowly made it back to normal. My spiritual life spiraled upward. I began playing in churches again and studying the Bible. Then suddenly I was diagnosed with heart disease which I have struggled with mightily for many years.

Yet there were so many good and usually unexpected things that happened. I was blessed with the chance to live in Italy for a year, I discovered the joy of wilderness fishing and took over thirty-five fishing/camping trips to Canada—a special joy to me! When I met my husband I quit my tenured faculty position in a university in my home town of Atlanta to move to the state and city where my husband taught. In a time when college teaching positions were few and hard to obtain, I was asked to join the faculty of the very school where my husband was employed—even without applying for the job! We worked together there until retirement whereupon I began writing creatively. My first novel won a contest and was published. I know now that the Lord laid out my path and has been with me through it all. I am reminded of the words of Ugo Betti: "To believe in God is to know that He is, and that there will be wonderful surprises." Bad things continue to happen but always mixed in are moments of great joy and those "wonderful surprises."

People ask me what denomination I adhere to and my answer is I belong to God and any church that worships Jesus is my church. As a pianist and organist I have had the opportunity to play in just about every denomination of Christian church. There is good in all. Officially I have been a Presbyterian, a Pentecostal, a Baptist, and finally a Roman Catholic. I love the ritual of the Mass, especially the Eucharist. Occasionally I will attend a Church of God or Assembly of God for the praise and worship or an Episcopal church for the elegance of the service and the classical organ music.

You will find traces of my spiritual journey in these verses, perhaps traces of your own pilgrimage. My prayer is that each reader will find a few poems that minister to them and help them celebrate God's Word and our Christian faith. The illustrations are taken from my computer's collection of "clip art." Poems with a little musical eighth note by the title have been set to music.

Each poem is imbued with a humble but fervent prayer in the intent that some of them may give you strength in weakness, faith in doubt, hope in despair, and love when you feel without it.

May God bless you abundantly and hold you close under His wings of love and mercy forever.

Judith Barban

P.S. – Though it's a long way from polished, the poetry set to music can be yours, but you need to act fast. For a limited time, if you will post a review of this book at Amazon.com, email me a copy of that review (it can be positive or negative) and we will send you a flash drive with the music on it. Contact me at barbanj@comporium.net.

For my mother, Mary Lucinda Hall Clark, who gave me my first Bible and encouraged me to read it in prayer daily. She never consoled, counseled or reprimanded me and my sisters without quoting a passage from the Old or New Testament as confirmation. She had a beautiful voice and always sang hymns while doing the work of full-time housewife and mother. Despite the many hardships she had to endure, she lived a joyful Christian life all of her 101 years!! A poem I wrote about her appears on the next page.

Mama

I have seen Him in a face
whose eyes radiant with love
and smile of gentle grace
bring the gift of joy

I have heard Him in a voice
like a cooling stream
that slakes the heart's thirst
teaches the wisdom of laughter

I have felt Him in a presence
more potent than any medicine
just to know "She is here!"
imparts hope and healing

I have watched Him in a life
of sacrifice and selfless tears
shining with heaven's beauty
and love beyond measure

When that day comes, face to His face
I will recognize a friend
an old familiar warmth
for I have known Him, Mama, in you

Author's Note:
This poem about my mother appeared in
Crown Jewels, published in 2014.

"Have no anxiety about anything, but in everything by prayer and supplication with thanksgiving let your requests be made known to God."

Philippians 4:6 (RSV)

Poems of
Petition and Supplication

Breathing
A Meditation before Prayer

breathe in
breathe out

breathe in calm
breathe out clamor

breathe in forgiveness
breathe out resentment

breathe in mercy
breathe out revenge

breathe in joy
breathe out sorrow

breathe in serenity
breathe out bitterness

breathe in harmony
breathe out discord

breathe in hope
breathe out fear

breathe in trust
breathe out doubt

breathe in truth
breathe out deceit

breathe in peace
breathe out turmoil

breathe in the Spirit of God
breathe out the spirit of evil

breathe in Jesus
breathe out everything else

Lord, You Know How It Is

A Preamble to the Lord's Prayer

Lord, You know how it is
down here
on earth
You lived among us
experienced the good and the bad
life has to offer
some believed You, loved You
some discounted You, hated You

it's the same for us, for me

You suffered
physical pain
endured disappointment
grew angry at greed
wept at the loss of a friend
were betrayed by another

it's the same for us, for me

You went about doing
what was expected of You
You knew
from the beginning
You would have to die

it's the same for us, for me

To get through it all
You prayed with fervor
so do we, so do I
in your words:

Our Father . . .

The Lord's Prayer

Matthew 6: 9 - 13

Our Father
Which art in heaven
Hallowed be thy name

Thy kingdom come
Thy will be done in earth
As it is in heaven

Give us this day our daily bread
And forgive us our debts
As we forgive our debtors

And lead us not into temptation
But deliver us from evil

For thine is the kingdom
and the power, and the glory forever

Amen

Come, Lord

Come, Lord
In Your glory
In Your power
Banish evil
From the earth
Fill the universe
With Your presence
With Your peace

Come, Lord
Imbue each human heart
With Your love
Make it pure
Make it holy
Make every one
A channel
Of Your Spirit

Come, Lord
To Your creation
Restore us to the Garden
Where we can walk
Without sin
Without shame
In harmony with You
In the cool of the evening

Lamb of God ♪

Lamb of God
Blessed Sacrifice
Son of God
Joy of Paradise

You take away
The sins of the world
Have mercy on us

Bread of Life
Offering of grain
As we come
Feed us once again

You take away
The sins of the world
Have mercy on us

Lamb of God
Blessed sacrifice
Son of God
Joy of Paradise

You take away
The sins of the world
Grant us peace

This poem is a version of the *Agnus Dei* from the Roman Catholic *Mass of the Holy Trinity* composed by Judith Barban

Let Your Glorylight Shine

Let your glorylight shine
the beauty and sweetness
power and majesty of Jesus

Let your glorylight shine
the wonder of your love
compassion and forgiveness

Let your glorylight shine
the warmth and healing
saving grace and peace

Let your glorylight shine
on all the broken hearts
on all the broken lives

on all this broken world
merciful Lord I pray
Let your glorylight shine

In the Name of Jesus

In the name of Jesus
I would preach the gospel
feed the hungry
clothe the naked
shelter the homeless
be a parent to orphans
care for widows
forgive my enemies
love the unlovely
do good for evil

In the name of Jesus
I would be
a giver to the poor
a friend to the lonely
a peacemaker in conflicts
a helper in times of need

In the name of Jesus
I would be always
generous

thoughtful

kind

loving

calm

soft-spoken

In the name of Jesus

I would do and be

many things

but I am only me

limited in so many ways

Empower me, Lord

I pray

in the name of Jesus

The Meeting Place

I come alone to kneel and pray
the way You did in the Garden
of Gethsemane
to our meeting place
with praise for Your holiness
thanksgiving for Your grace
after all my petitions are made
I wait to see if You will join me
at the meeting place

My human eyes cannot see You
my human ears cannot hear You
my human hands cannot touch You
most times I have no sense
of any Holy Presence
saints nor angels
seraphim nor cherubim
I linger, seeking Your face
at the meeting place

I rise, I go my way
thinking "He didn't show today"
and turn away to daily chores
then when I least expect it
a little clue, a subtle hint
drops into my life—
a call from a forgotten friend,
a check in the mail
an unexplained coincidence—

I know at once You heard
every word, You did not fail
to receive my prayer
at the meeting place

No Matter What

Let me live
in the presence
of God

Every breath an
intake of His Spirit
every heartbeat a
thank-you
thank-you
thank-you
Je-sus

Let me rejoice and sing
"Alleluia"
in my soul
always
no matter what
no matter what

Poet's Prayer

Psalm 139.2 NIV

I cannot hide from You, Lord
You know
when I sit
when I stand
when I walk
when I run

You sense every feeling
and its source
You are aware of every thought
before I think it
even the deep ones hidden to me

I am open before You
cleanse me like a goblet
remove every spot
wash me like a garment
remove every stain
revise me like a poem

A Prayer for Healing

You spoke into being
all of creation
You made humans
in your very image
body-mind-spirit
three in one

as such I come to You
Jesus-God-Holy Spirit
to ask, to seek, to knock
at the door of Heaven
for healing
believing your promise
to receive, to find
to have your compassion
opened to *me*

find your way through
the complicated composition
of neurons and nodes
the complex chemistry
of brain and blood
the miracles and mysteries
as yet hidden to science.

touch *me* with your power
touch *me* with your love

and *I* shall be healed in
body, mind, and spirit.

This poem can be used to pray for anyone
by substituting the person's name for "me" and "I."

Cocoon

Envelope me, Lord
spin silken threads
of your Spirit around me
create a sacred cocoon

Cleanse me, Lord
of any impurity
in what I say or do
within this cocoon

Nourish me, Lord
with the wisdom
of your word
within this cocoon

Comfort me, Lord
soothe the aches
of my mind and heart
within this cocoon

Protect me, Lord
from evil enticements
the snares of Satan
within this cocoon

Teach me, Lord
to pray to You

to hear your voice
within this cocoon

Strengthen me, Lord
let me grow in love
for all your creation
within this cocoon

Receive me, Lord
when with glistening wings
I emerge and fly to You
from this cocoon

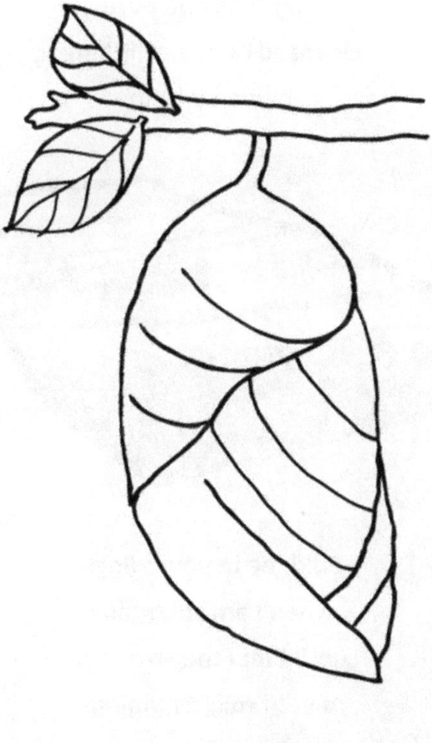

Cover Me with a Blanket

Cover me with a blanket
of your goodness and mercy
Let the warmth of your love seep
deep into my soul

Hover over me in the cloud
of your glory
until I shine forth
your light into the darkness

Bathe me in your holiness
that I may be pure
cleansed of any evil thing
hidden within

Fold me in your wings
when I am struggling
until I feel the strength
of your mighty pinions

Fill my heart
with the song of angels
then joy and praise
will flood my being

The Basket

The tears of my heart
The pain of my body
The worries of my mind
The plan-to-do list
The failed-to-do list
Regret
Remorse
Inadequacies
I place them all
in a basket of faith
and lift them up to
You

As You reach to take my
basket of burdens
Let Your Healing Hands
touch mine

Bless the Tears

Bless the tears shed
in worship of You
Consider them droplets
of holy water
that flow in gratitude for
your so great love
your so amazing grace
a stream of adoration
an offering of praise

May your Holy Angels
collect them
and bear them as gifts
to lay before your throne

Empty Me

Empty me, O God
of worry
of worldly matters
great and small

Empty me of plans
things I want to do
things I think
I ought to do

Empty me of fear
that something
may go wrong
that I will not be strong

Empty me of self
how I look
how I feel
even who I am

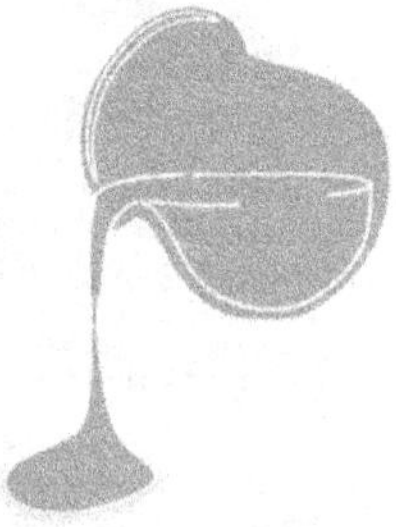

Empty me, O God
unclog my carnal mind
cleanse me wholly
make me pure

Then
Stream of Living Water
Fill me

Symphony

Orchestrate my life, Lord
in major mode or minor
make me many instruments
strings of soft worship
woodwinds of perfect peace
horns of majestic glory
a symphony of salvation

Stand on the podium before me
I will fix my eyes on You
watching for your cue to play
strings
woodwinds
or horns
at times let the percussion
celebrate Your greatness
Your infinite power and love

And I will play Your music
until strands of its healing harmony
reach every heart
in need of You.

Shell Poem

I am but an empty shell
hollow
needing to be filled

not with earthly distractions
family
friends
how-to-do's
ought-to-do's
worry

pour Your Spirit into me
--unworthy as I am—
like a precious healing oil
bring Life to
the void
inside me

set me anew
in the Sea of Life

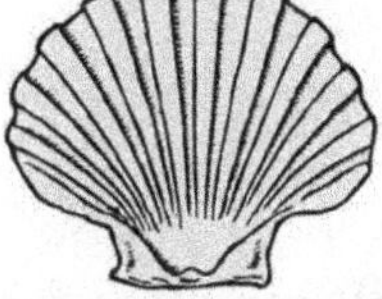

Hymn to the Cross

Cross of Jesus
Lift me

lift me from sin
raise me to righteousness

lift me from doubt
raise me to faith

lift me from sorrow
raise me to joy

lift me from worry
raise me to peace

lift me from fear
raise me to trust

lift me from hate
raise me to love

lift me from death
raise me to life

Prayer When All Else Fails

I

I am here
kneeling, praying
You are there
Somewhere

I am here
weeping, seeking
You are there
Somewhere

II

Doubt
has wormed its way
into my mind
is eating at the fiber of my
Faith

Despair
has settled deep inside
my soul
its weight pounding away at my
Heart

III

Jesus

to whom is given all

Power

come to mend my thread-bare cloak of

Hope

Jesus

who endured the cross and rose from

Death

make my heart sing again great canticles of

Praise

Prayer When the End Is Near ♪

All I want is
Jesus
To praise his holy name
Forever
To walk away from
Time
And the
Human Condition
And live in the presence of
God
Forever in the presence of
God *

* Repeat (or sing) this last phrase until peace and acceptance settle in your heart.

"Enter into his gates with thanksgiving and into his courts with praise:
be thankful unto him and bless his name."
Psalm 100: 4

Poems of Thanksgiving, Praise, and Worship

Call to Worship ♪

Royal Preisthood

Holy Nation

Worship the Father

Worship the Son

Worship the Holy Spirit

Come and praise the Lord our God

Come and glorify Jesus His Son

Come receive the Holy One

Who lives within our hearts

If I Had a Thousand Voices

If I had a thousand voices
I would sing your praises
in such richly-woven textures
shining harmonies
complex counterpoints
as to astonish angels
majestic melodies would
rise and fall
in crescendos and diminuendos
an ocean of glorious sound

I have but one voice
a monody that wanes
too soon
faint and pale
its limited range
unworthy of great arias
repentant, sincere
weeping, hoping
its music will reach
your infinite ear

The Sign of the Cross

In the name of the Father

I touch my forehead
where I know your story
the Creation and fall
the enslavement of your people
the wanderings,
the promised land
judges, kings, and prophets
the birth, teachings, healings
death and resurrection
of Jesus, God in flesh

and of the Son

I touch my navel
symbol of your gift
of human life to us
and to your only Son
nourishment then separation
life in the womb
becomes life in the world
search for a new source
of sustenance and safety
warmth of love
I have drawn a vertical line
down the center of my body

and of the Holy Spirit

I touch one shoulder
then the other
limbs of the body
arms and legs
that work to spread the gospel
that walk the Way of the Lord
whether in the pulpit
mission field,
hospital, market, home
with family, friends, strangers

I have drawn a horizontal line
across my chest

The two lines intersect
over my heart
the dwelling place of
Father, Son, and Holy Spirit
one God forever and ever
Amen

JESUS ♪

You are Jesus

the Holy One

You are Jesus

God's only son

You are Jesus

the bright morning star

You are Jesus

the Lamb of God

You are Jesus

the prince of peace

You are Jesus

the king of kings

You are Jesus

the fairest of ten thousand

You are Jesus

the Lamb of God

You are Jesus

Lion of Judah

You are Jesus

the Word made flesh

You are Jesus

Alpha and Omega

You are Jesus

the Lamb of God

Worship

to God
praise
glory
honor
thanksgiving

not for favors
not for rewards
not for points in heaven

but because of
who you are
the Almighty
the Holy One
Giver of everything good

The Name of Jesus ♪

The name of Jesus
is holy
He is the King of Glory
I praise Him

The name of Jesus
is healing
He is the King of Glory
I praise Him

The name of Jesus
is mighty
He is the King of Glory
I praise Him

Jesus Savior
I love You
You are the King of Glory
I love You Lord

Holy Lord ♪

Holy Lord
I praise your name
Holy Lord
I praise your name
for your Cross
freed me from sin
Holy Lord
I worship You

Holy Lord
I praise your name
Holy Lord
I praise your name
for your Light
shines in my soul
Holy Lord
I worship You

Holy Lord
I praise your name
Holy Lord
I praise your name
for your Love
has filled my heart

Holy Lord

I worship You

In Silence

Today
I wait
I kneel
in silence
before You

Thanksgiving seeps out slowly
unspoken but felt
gratitude for life
for breath
for a beating heart

Family, friends
food, shelter, sufficiency
love, laughter
You have given me
everything that is good

I remember the many
who hunger and thirst
who suffer
who mourn
who seek Your face

As I wait

and kneel

in silence

before You

Almighty God

Holy Presence

There is one thing I seek, Lord
with all my heart
with all my mind
with all my soul
with all my strength

There is one thing that I need, Lord
more than food
more than water
more that shelter
more than air to breathe

There is one thing that I desire
above riches
above fame
above intelligence
above health

Yet I do not know
where I might find
this one thing that I seek
that I need
that I desire

Your Holy Presence
which is the living water
the bread of life
joy unspeakable and
full of glory

Come, Lord
bestow on me this precious gift
unworthy as I am
surround me, fill me with
Your Holy Presence

Then I will
glorify You
praise you
worship You
in the beauty of Holiness

Straying Away

I know I stray
from You
a little every day
pulled away by
responsibilities
commitments to
family, friends, work
distracted by
telephones, television
emails, duties of all kinds
that take time
I would rather spend
with You

But in the quiet moments
in the solitude of the night
Your love calls me back
draws me near
'till beneath me I feel
the Everlasting Arms

You Are There

You are there
somewhere
not a comic book king
on a throne in the sky
You are a Force
a positive force
a creative force
a propelling force
the *élan vital*
pushing each creation
more and more
into life

At some point
You withdraw that force
the waxing is over
the waning begins
You are another Force
equally strong
a counterbalance
not a negative but
a drawing force
pulling each creation
more and more
back to You

Totally Yours

Totally Yours, Lord
I am totally Yours
at times the enemy
had me in his grasp
made me do things
though I knew better
put thoughts and desires
in my head
made me act
according to his will

But I fought
as best I could
to find the way
back to You
slowly but surely
back to You
through pain
through darkness
through sleepless nights
back to You, Lord

Now I sing praises
to your Holy Name
I will forever remain

totally Yours, Lord

totally Yours

I Want to Walk in the Presence of God

I want to walk in the presence of God
every step
wherever I go
however I travel
that Divine Love may accompany me

I want to stay in the presence of God
never looking away
never falling away
nor going astray
that Divine Light may shine though me

I want to live in the presence of God
a life free of sin
a life of unselfishness
a life of forgiveness
that Divine Mercy may be shown

I want to be in the presence of God
at all times
in all places
in all circumstances
that Divine Holiness will radiate from me

I want to rejoice in the presence of God

with thanksgiving in my soul
and halleluiah in my heart
happiness an aura around me
that Divine Joy will spill over

I want to sing in the presence of God
a new song of praise
to magnify
the name of the Lord
in Divine Worship before the throne

I want to die in the presence of God
relinquish my dreams
release my hopes
return my life
that Divine Praise will flow from me forever

Softly

Softly, softly
my heart speaks to You
in words of love
a sacred language of its own

quiet words
of beauty and peace
that still the noisy world
around me

sealed within those
gentle words
the strength of faith
the force of joy

erupt into silent praise
glorifying your name
all within my heart
as I go about the day

Seeking Definition

the loftiest thoughts
the deepest dreams
cannot reach
the grandeur
the greatness of
God

no sermon or song
no portrait or poem
can ever define
the infinite
God

Kaleidoscope

When I look down the shadowy corridor of
time past
I see bits and pieces of my life
broken, chaotic
formless, coated in shades of gray by
faulty memory
sadness, embarrassment, failure stand out
above all
I despair

But when I raise my eye-on-the-past to
your Light
the fragments take a multitude of
geometric shapes
vibrant colors that dazzle my vision
perfect symmetry
that makes sense of it all and floods
my heart
with gratitude for your design
I rejoice

All

You're all I want
You're all I need
You're everything to me

All my achievements
All my treasures
All my earthly attachments

I lay before You. They are
ashes blown away
by eternal winds into nothingness

I surrender all to You, Savior
my body, my mind, my spirit
I place on the altar of sacrifice

Your presence
Your mercy
Your love
my all

You Are My God

I can't see You
yet I seek Your face
I can't hear You
but You speak to my heart
I can't touch You
though I feel Your presence

You are my God

so many miracles
You have wrought
in my life
rescued me from death
that I surely deserved
given me moments of joy
that obscured the sorrow

You are my God

I know
Your hand is leading
I know
Your Word is speaking
I know
Your love is everlasting

You are my God

Identity

You are Creator

I am created

You are Everything

I am nothing

You are Peace

I am struggle

You are All That Matters

I am insignificant

You are Eternal

I am ephemeral

You are Redeemer

I am redeemed

How ♪

I want to worship You
I want to praise You

Teach me how, Lord
Teach me how

I want to follow You
I want to serve You

Show me the way, Lord
Show me the way

I want to honor You
I want to love You more

Open my heart, Lord
Open my heart

Each step, each breath
Each heartbeat

Let it be for You, Lord
Let it be for You

Searching

Who can know the mind of God
to think as the Omniscient thinks
to see past present and future
as one and the same?

Who can even begin
to explain the Omnipotent
Creator of the infinitely
great and small?

Those who have believed Him
those who have received Him
have no need to know
or to explain

Trying

all sermons spoken
all hymns sung
all rhymes written
try to describe You

all prayers uttered
all cries raised
all hopes whispered
try to reach You

all heads bowed
all knees bent
all hands raised
try to worship You

all verses read
all psalms repeated
all scriptures studied
try to understand You

all tears shed
all penance done
all confessions made
try to appease You

all seems in vain

all falls short

all ends in silence

perhaps trying is enough

Stranger

At times the world consumes me
I drown in a sea of
conflict, confusion
misunderstandings, unfairness
hate, violence
crime, drugs
grief, pain

How blessed are the moments
when my path crosses
a stranger who knows You
who speaks your name to me
and in that moment my spirit
rises in joyous hope
above the world
above it all

to You who have
overcome the world

Giver of Life

You knitted me together
from sperm and egg
and every cell thereafter

a complex body
you created around
a beating heart

emerging with clenched fists
I reached for the world
cried out, thirsted for it all

body and mind expanding
in the early years
I learned the meaning of tears

tasted the sweetness of pleasure
the bitterness of pain
against the palate of my soul

searching everywhere for treasure
I found You, Lord
or maybe You found me

who finally realized
I always was
and ever will be Yours

Glory Drops

"what they say"
what I think

recovery from illness

"the medicine worked"

no, a glory drop fell

landing a great job

"you deserved it"

no, a glory drop fell

an unexpected promotion

"you worked hard for it"

no, a glory drop fell

a problem solved

"you figured it out"

no, a glory drop fell

a narrow escape

"you were lucky"

no, a glory drop fell

a reversal of fortune

"what a coincidence"

no, a glory drop fell

so many glory drops

have fallen in my life

yet I long for the

pouring rain

of Your Spirit

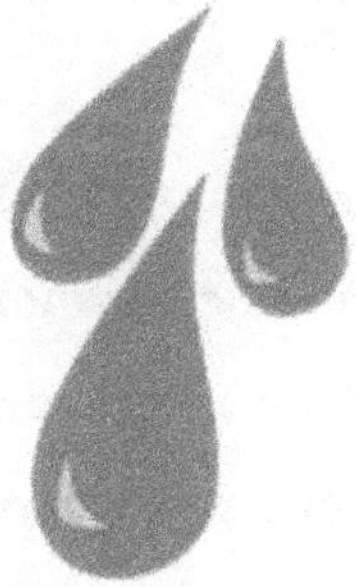

The Eucharist

(Loosely based on the hymn "Pan de Vida" by Bob Hurd, Pia Mioratti, and Jaime Cortez)

Holy wafer, sacred wine
Bread of Life, body divine
pan de vida, cuerpo del Señor
Cup of blessing, blood of *Cristo redentor*

I eat, I drink—I consume
the One by whom
I am consumed
ever wanting more
of the *santa copa*

Eyes closed, mind quiet
I speak the words, "I am
not worthy that you should enter . . .
I open to see there before me
the cross
the Holy Cross
the dying Lord

and I grieve
for my own sins
for the sins of the world
which your cross can take away
I open my heart to receive

power to serve

poder es servir

God who is love

porque Dios es amor

Love one another as I have loved you

**"Thy word is a lamp unto my feet
and a light unto my path."**
Psalm 119: 105

Poems for Biblical Reflection

Prayer before Reading the Bible

As I open the Holy Book
let the eyes of my heart
perceive your truth
let the hunger of my mind
receive your wisdom
I would eat
the bread of life
I would drink
the wine of your Word
each verse a wafer
each chapter a cup
I would partake
until filled
with your presence
I enter into
full communion with You
my Redeemer
and my God

The Old Testament

THE TORAH

Genesis, Exodus, Leviticus,

Numbers, Deuteronomy

Genesis Chapter 1

a rushing wind
sweeps over the waters

the Voice speaks

a primal brightness
dispells the darkness

the Voice speaks

wild beasts roar
cattle low

birds on the wing
snakes in a crawl

all multiply
fill the earth

only one creature
upright

standing tall
can know

when evening comes
morning will follow

Exodus

Israelites in battle array
peasants, slaves
backs to Egypt
march behind their leader
toward the Red Sea
carrying their brother's bones

Moses follows the Lord
a column of cloud
the Shekinah Glory
by day shows the way
so they can journey on

They travel in darkness
the Lord bright
in a column of fire
lights the path by night
toward miracles to come

A wall of water on each side
they pass through
on dry ground
then watch the currents resume
and their enemies drown

Water spurts from a rock
bread appears in the dew
quails fall from the sky
yet they bicker and complain

fashion a god in animal form

On Sinai's mountain
the weary Man intercedes
before Yahweh
saving them from the wrath
that would destroy the Chosen Ones

Day and night they move
with fear of God, faith in His man
through hostile land
the glorious columns never failing
leads them home

SEEKING HIS FACE

Deuteronomy 4:29; 6:5; also Jeremiah 29:13

You have blessed me
in so many ways
in the days of my youth
in the days of my later years
yet one thing I have not found
but have sought with
all my heart and
all my soul
Your Face, Most Holy Lord

We are told
we cannot see your face and live
we are told
we will find it through
seeking
how will I know
when I have found You?
how will I recognize
Your countenance?
Must I first pass through
the Dark Sea of Death?

I shall continue by faith
ever seeking You

ever loving You

with all my mind , soul, and strength

until the last heartbeat

erases my existence on the earth

opens my spiritual eyes

and lifts me to behold You

face to Face

Leviticus

My laws
enscribed in stone
on two tablets
in the Holy Place
beneath the wings
of the cherubim
and those
delivered to Israel
from Moses through Aaron
on cleanliness, mercy
justice, sacrifice
honesty, purity

by obedience
would make you holy
like I AM

wayward children,
weak and wandering,
I will write them
in My Blood
on your hearts

Prayer for a Blessing
Numbers 6: 24-27

Father of peace, Father of love
pour forth your blessings upon me
even though I have sinned
remember them no more
keep me safe from harm
keep me close to You
let the light of Your countenance
shine on me always
be gracious to me, O Lord
grant me Your peace all along
the difficult journey of life
may your Name be upon me
forever

Just as Aaron was taught
to bless the children of Israel
so this prayer is offered up to You

This prayer may be used to pray for others.
Simply substitute the words "me" and "I" with the person's name.

HISTORY

Joshua, Judges, Ruth, 1st + 2nd Samuel, 1st Kings, 1st+ 2nd Chronicles, Esther

Joshua

Successor of Moses
he heard the command
to meditate on the Book
of the Law, to obey
to remain
courageous and fearless
he believed
the Lord would be
with him,
never fail him
never forsake him

On the banks of the river
he commanded the priests
to enter the water
bearing the arc
to stand still in the midst
while he and the Israelites
crossed the Jordan
on dry ground
to the promised land
wherever he walked
God's gift to Israel

He conquered kings

took possession of cities

he did not build

vineyards he did not plant

gave each tribe a homeland

in which to rest

Joshua chose

to serve the Lord

Deborah and Jael
Judges Chapters 4 and 5

Deborah the prophetess
dwelt under a palm
in the time of Jabin
king of Canaan
oppressor of Israel
and Sisera his
warrior, feared leader
with nine hundred
chariots of iron

Directed by God
she summoned
Barak, Israelite champion
ordered him to march
out to meet Sisera, his army
and chariots of iron
With Deborah by his side
Barak defeated the army
and the nine hundred
chariots of iron

But Sisera fled
took refuge instead
and slept

in the tent of Heber
and his wife Jael
With hammer in one hand
tent peg in the other
Jael drove the stake
into the head of Sisera
warrior with nine hundred
chariots of iron

Deborah and Barak
sang together
a victory song
of deliverance
by the Lord
by Deborah
by Barak
and by Jael
whose simple hands
destroyed Sisera
warrior with nine hundred
chariots of iron

Naomi and Ruth
The Book of Ruth

Famine in Judah drove
a husband and his wife
Naomi
with two sons
into heathen land
Moab
where the husband died
the sons took wives
but died in their youth
Naomi
bereft and grieving
took leave of her
daughters-in-law
Orpah
loved but stayed
Ruth
loved but followed
accepting a new people and the
God of Israel

Two women on the road to
Bethlehem
Naomi to her people
Ruth

to her great destiny

gleaning in the fields of

Boaz

by whom she gave birth to

Obed

whose son was

Jesse

the father of the great king

David

then in fourteen generations

the birth in that royal city of the

King of Kings

Your Voice
I Samuel 3:1 – 10; also I Kings 19: 11 - 13

There is a multitude of earthly voices

many so beautiful
they are thought to be Your Voice
a wren's shrill song
a child's innocent laughter
a loved one's tender words

many so powerful
they are thought to be Your Voice
the boom of a jarring thunderclap
the roar of a turbulent sea
the whir of hurricane winds

many so kind
they are thought to be Your Voice
a stranger's "I'll pay that for you"
a friend's "Let me help you"
a parent's "I forgive you"

But Your Voice is
a calling
a calling to listen
a calling to obey
a still small voice

calling in the night

and we answer

"Speak, Lord, for Your servant is listening,"

Building the House of the Lord Today

I Chronicles 28: 20

at times I am afraid
often dismayed
by what I hear and see
in the world around me
my hope wanes
while evil reigns
I feel helpless and weak
when the future looks bleak

but You, oh Lord
my courage and strength
give me length
of days to do Your will
and with Your spirit fill
this servant however frail
whom you will not forsake or fail

Jahoshaphat's Prayer before the Assembly of Judah
2nd Chronicles 20:12

There are so many times
when I don't know
what to do
to stop someone's pain
to remedy a bad situation
to untie the knots
of evil which bind
a friend
a parent
a child

So my eyes are always on You
who have the power
to end suffering
to solve dilemmas
to set the captives free

Esther

In royal robes
she stood uninvited
before the king
willing to die for daring

orphaned as a child
raised by Mordecai
chosen from the harem
to be queen

She voiced her proposal
"I will prepare a feast
for you and Haman
your right-hand man"

Pouring the king's wine
she whispered in his ear
"Remember Mordecai the Jew
saved you from assassins

now Haman plans to slaughter
every Jew of your realm
including Mordecai
and your queen"

He has cast the *pur*

to decide the date
I beg you, act now
before it is too late"

the queen's convincing words
reversed the role of fortune
Mordecai was acclaimed
while Haman was hanged

Through the years
even today
***Purim* celebrates a people's freedom**
and the courage of one beauty queen

POETRY

Selections from

Job, Psalms, Proverbs, Ecclesiastes

God's Hands
Job 5:18

I have placed my life
in your hands, Lord
the potter's formless clay
the sculptor's rough stone
the poet's blank page
an instrument waiting
for You to play

Your right hand
holds mine
its warm and steadfast grip
comforts me
soothes my spirit
assures me
calms my heart

Your left hand
shows the way ahead
commands my attention
indicates dangers
points out solutions
keeps me alert
to temptation

Your hands

at times reprove

my errant ways

wound me

then bind me up

strike then heal

my repentant heart

Psalm 91:5

Let me be aware of your presence
all the time
open the door that leads
from your spirit
from your wisdom
from your power
from your goodness
to my heart

Keep it open at all times
lest I forget
lest I stray
lest I say or do
something wrong
something unlike You

With the sense of your nearness
all the time
I will walk secure
I will not fear
the terrors of the night
nor the arrow that flies by day

In the Shadow of Your Wings ♪
Psalm 36: 7

In the shadow of Your wings
I find a hiding place
There with all my heart
I seek Your face
and I know
You will keep me safe
in the shadow of Your wings

Heart Medicine
Proverbs 12:25 and 17:22

people, God's people

weighed down by

anxiety

burdened by

circumstances

in their lives

downcast in spirit

worried about

money

relationships

job security

health

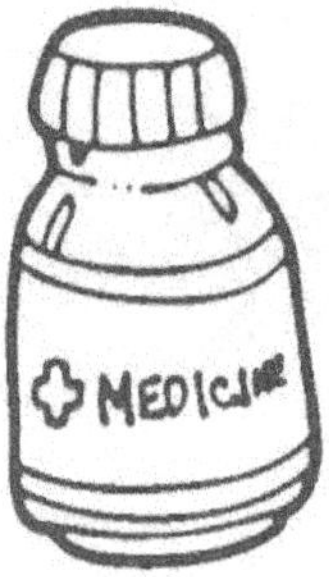

it is human

natural instinct

but it is not

God's way

a smile, a laugh

a pleasant word

spoken in joy

will lift up

cheer and heal like

medicine for the heart

The Tower
Proverbs 18:10

I cannot fathom
the immensity of your being
the breadth of your knowledge
the depth of your gaze
into the hearts of your creatures
your infiniteness
your omnipotence
your completeness
astound me
I fear your displeasure
revere your holiness
worship your divinity
take refuge in your name:
Yahweh, Yessua, Jesus
it is a strong tower
I run into it
and I am safe
filled with your peace
enveloped in
your infiniteness
your omnipotence
your completeness

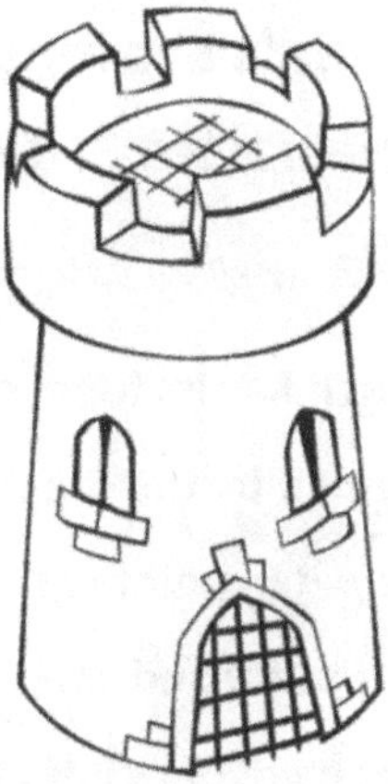

JEHOVAH

God's Seasons
Ecclesiastes 3: 1 – 8

The earth has its four seasons
framed by the Creator
portrayed in paintings, music
poetry and song
we have our clothing
suited to each
windows to watch the changes
furnaces, fireplaces
air conditioners, ceiling fans
skiing, swimming
hiking, hunting
activities adapted
a time for each

Life has its four seasons, too
framed by the Creator
we pass unheeding
from one to the next
childhood
a season to laugh and play
young adulthood
a season to dance and sing
maturity
a season to build up

seek and speak up

sunset years

a season of slowing down

mourning lost loved ones

understanding the meaning

silent death

and

joyful rebirth

to life pure and eternal

Trust
Proverbs 3: 5-6

No way out
No solution possible
Hopeless situation
Might as well give up
I don't understand
how it got like this
I don't understand
why this had to happen

Forget efforts to find a way
Stop trying to understand why
Worrying will do no good
TRUST IN THE LORD
for there is a promise if you do:
HE WILL DIRECT YOUR PATHS
Cast away your fears
Calm the nervous worries
There is peace and assurance
for those who without any doubt
TRUST IN THE LORD

PROPHECY

Selections from

Isaiah, Jeremiah, Lamentations, Ezekiel, Hosea, Micah

Waiting
Isaiah 40:28

Since my earliest years
You have rescued me
again and again
from sin
physical harm
going my way
instead of Yours

Your instant answers
spoiled me
a tiny wish
immediately fulfilled
a hunger
suddenly satisfied
a whim
yes, even a whim
brought to fruition

Now this request
far greater than any
no quick volley
no fast reprieve
no sign of relief
are the eyes and ears of heaven

closed?

You are the Everlasting God

Creator of the ends of the earth

unlike me

You do not faint or grow weary

I will wait for Your answer

as long as it takes

God's Promises
Jeremiah Chapters 30 and 31

You spoke
through the prophet
Jeremiah
and promised
to save us
to restore our health
to heal our wounds
to be our God
to love us
with an everlasting love
to turn our mourning into joy
to give us gladness for sorrow
to refresh the weary among us

to let us all
know You
who You are
what You are
how great You are

Prayer and Patience
Lamentations Chapters 2 and 3

when circumstances steal my peace
happiness seems an illusion
at night my thoughts focus on unjust fate
sleep cannot cover my eyes
my bed is soft my mind is hard
I arise and come to You, my God
I pour out my heart like water
I remember your steadfast love
your mercy does not wear thin
it is there new every morning
You are faithful to souls who seek You
to those who wait before You
I will see your salvation
if I wait quietly, patiently for You

New
Ezekiel 36: 24 - 28

I want to be

new

inside and out

where does outside end

inside begin?

emotions tied to heart

mind tied to brain

all connected

mind, spirit, body

head knowledge, heart knowledge

one conscious, one subconscious

both in the mind-brain

You promise a new heart

a new spirit to

all who

believe in You

ask your forgiveness

follow You

obey your commands

love You

In this very moment

I present to You

Jesus Savior and God

my body-mind-heart-spirit

open and poured out

make it new

make it like You

Return to the LORD
Hosea 14:7; Joel 2:12 – 13; Malachi 3:7

I have been traveling with you, Lord
for some time now
occasionally our paths have divided
I veered, lured by life's attractions
beckoned by "give it a try," it'll be fun,"
"everyone's doing it," "you'll love it!"
so I gave it a try
it was fun, everyone was doing it
I did love it
yet in the middle of things
a song, a scene, a story
something touched my spirit
reminded me of You
drew me back to the journey
our paths connected again

The joy, the greatness, the glory
of that rejoining
You are always there, unchanged
loving and forgiving
this weak and wandering soul

Your Presence ♪
Micah 7:8
also 2 Samuel 22: 29

Your Presence, Lord
is all I need
to keep my heart in perfect peace

Your presence, Lord
is all I need
Your Holy Spirit will guide me

Your presence, Lord
will see me through my darkest night
Your hand in mine
Your love divine
my only light

THE NEW TESTAMENT

Selections from the Gospels including

The Acts of the Apostles

Selections from the Epistles of Saint Paul

and

The Epistles of James, Peter, and John

The Revelation of Saint John

The Child
Matthew 18: 1 - 4

The child came to Jesus
meek
innocent
obedient
quiet
respectful
attentive
to his words

"To enter the Kingdom
be like this little one"
He said
So we come to Jesus
meek
humble before Him
innocent
forgiven of sin
obedient
to his commandments
quiet
listening for his voice
respectful
before the Holy One

attentive

to his Word

Like the child, Lord

we come to You

Jesus Only
Mark 9: 7 - 8

Lead me to the mountain top
Let the cloud come down

Let the glory of God shine

Let the voice speak

Let me hear

Let me see

Not Peter, James, or John

Not Moses, not Elijah

No one but the "Beloved Son"

No one but Jesus only

All my life

Always Jesus only

Handmaid of the Lord
Luke 1:26-38

Sent from God the angel came
to Nazareth
to a young virgin
to foretell her future

Frightened, confused
she listened
as he predicted
an out-of-wedlock child

a terrible thing
sure rejection
by her betrothed
sure death by stoning

Submissive she spoke
"I am the handmaid of the Lord.
Let it be done to me
according to what you say."

My heart cries out
those very words
whatever you put upon me
I may not understand

Like Mary I am

the handmaid of the Lord

knowing there will be a Cross

but after that the Glory

The Kingdom of God ♪

The Kingdom of God
is within me
the Lord has made my heart
a dwelling place

I live every moment
by His Grace

and pray the I may
a servant be

I AM . . .
John Chapter 14

... the way

to forgiveness

to purity

to wisdom

to love

...the truth

about creation

about mercy

about peace

about love

...the life

in this world

in the next

in the Spirit

in love

I AM

the way to God

the truth of God

the life in God

Peter
Acts 5: 12 – 16

A fisherman

he followed

the son of

God

A simple man

he walked

trusting in

God

An empowered man

he spoke to crowds

about the mercy of

God

A holy man

he commanded evil

to flee before

God

A praying man

he healed the sick

in the name of

God

In Solomon's Portico

even his shadow

bestowed the power of

God

Can any obedient Christian

become a Peter

living in the Spirit of

God?

Two Laws
Romans Chapter 8

Here the apostle writes of
two laws
the law of Sin and Death
the law of Love and Life

the law of the Body
the law of the Spirit

the one esteems pleasure, power, possessions
the other values goodness, kindness, mercy

the one thinks only of self
the other puts everyone else first

the one seeks fame and fortune
the other seeks God

the one holds no lasting promise
the other promises everlasting life

Temple
I Corinthians 6:19-20

I lift my heart to You, Lord
look inside with your infinite vision
asses the damage with your perfect wisdom
repair what is broken
clean what is soiled
sew up what is torn
wipe away all bitterness
throw away any resentment

Make it pure

make it holy

make it worthy

to be a sanctuary

a temple of praise

to You

When the Heart Turns to the Lord
II Corinthians 3:12-18

When the heart turns to the Lord
the veil shall be taken away

we will see our sins
feel our nakedness
recognize our weakness
acknowledge our ignorance
sense our mortality

we will see a great light
sense the power
admire the beauty
revere the holiness
behold the glory of God

Conversation with the Lord about Love
II Corinthians Ch 13; Ephesians 5:25

Me: It seems there are two kinds of love
one on earth below and one in heaven above

Jesus: Don't let your imagination
confuse love with infatuation

Me: Our love begins with physical attraction
before it leads to any action

Jesus: Attraction plus something hidden deep
the first will fade, the second will keep

Me: Is there any way we humans can know
if what we feel will last and grow?

Jesus: Love is not based on what you feel
forgiveness and trust are signs it's real

Me: Sometimes even after long years
the love we had just disappears

Jesus: Love that's real will never die
but fill you more as time goes by

Me: When the beloved turns elsewhere
the pain is almost too much to bear

Jesus: I feel the same when you turn away
and forget me day after day

Me: So what you seem to explain
love is both sacred and profane

Jesus: Not so. True Love is divine
Both yours and mine.

Warrior
Ephesians 6: 11 - 18

Picture a Roman warrior
fully clad in metallic armor
helmet buckled under his chin
pauldrons on his shoulders
Sun glints off his breastplate
sword gleams in his right hand
his left arm bears
a shield emblazoned
with the fearsome letters
SPQR
The Senate and the Roman People
He stands on the battlefield
undaunted, knowing he will die

Picture the Christian warrior
dressed in the armor of God
the helmet of salvation
[we confess, He forgives][1]
loins girded with truth
[I AM the way, the truth, the life][2]
the breastplate of righteousness
[which comes from God by faith][3]

---

[1] I John 1:9
[2] John 14:6
[3] Romans 3:21-22

feet bringing the gospel of peace

[that is beyond understanding][4]

the shield of faith

[belief in God's mercy][5]

enscribed with INRI

Jesus of Nazareth King of the Jews

sword of the spirit, the word of God

with God in the beginning[6]

sharp, effective[7] never returns void[8]

He stands in the world

undaunted, knowing he will never die

---

4 Phil. 4:7

5 Ephes 2:4

6 John 1:1

7 Heb. 4:12

8 Isaiah 55:11

My Heart Is Worn
Galatians 6: 9

my heart is worn
pulsing tears of blood
through my vessels
where there once was
bright red joy
that lit my eyes
buoyed my step
lifted my spirit
high

prayers
pleading to be
restored
hang upon me
like a garland of chains
weighing me down
with the waiting
pulling
low

I grow weary
in well-doing
hoping not to faint
but reap in due season

Power
Philippians 4:13, 2 Corinthians 12:9 - 10

there is a power in the believer
not of the believer
but of God
from God
is God: the Holy Spirit

divine power
flows through a human channel
an open channel
unobstructed by pride
unhindered by vanity (ego, vainglory, selfishness)

the force that propels the flow
is life and death
a life in Christ
a death to self
unto life everlasting

Things Which Are Above
Colossians 3: 1 – 3

I am here on earth
moment by moment
day by day
week after week
months roll by
years pass
and it seems long

How can I keep my mind
on things which are above
which I have never seen
with my human eyes
only dimly
through a veil of *Faith*

When illness, tragedy
loss and grief beset
I call upon You
I concentrate on You
mind on things above
and You give me *Hope*
for better things below

In normal times
the daily grind

duties and tasks

open my spiritual eyes

to see clearly

your glory and goodness

everywhere, in everyone

let the mind of my heart

be always on You

and my life hid in your *Love*

The Will of God
! Thessalonians 5:16 – 18

Rejoice always ...
in gladness
in sadness
in love
in loss
in pleasant surprises
in disappointments

Pray without ceasing...
for those you love
for those you dislike
for those who help you
for those who hurt you
for those who serve God
for those who don't

Give thanks in all circumstances ...
when you win
when you lose
when it is given to you
when it is taken from you
when it goes well
when it doesn't

These three things

not easy to do

Do them anyway

For this is the will of God in Christ Jesus for you

God's Gifts
II Timothy 1:7

God has not given us
a spirit of fear
but of power
of love
of a sound mind.

Power
to spread the Good News

Love
to share with all

A sound mind
to understand His Word.

Morning Star Rising ♪
2 Peter 1.19

Morning Star
rising

rising from pain
rising from sorrow
rising from guilt

rising into repentance
rising into forgiveness
rising into joy

Morning Star
shining, a diadem
crowning my heart

shining in truth
shining in beauty
shining in love
shining in death

Alpha and Omega
Revelation 12:13 – 14

You are the *beginning*
my *first* love
You gave me new life
new hope of glory
new sustaining faith
through years of joy
and tears.

You are the *end*
my *last*ing love
light through the darkness
of the final hour
the light of glory
the brightness of heaven
and everlasting life.

OTHER BOOKS BY JUDITH BARBAN

Judith Barban joined the ThomasMax family in 2009 when her first novel, *Poplar River*, won the ThomasMax You Are Published prize at the Southeastern Writers Association's annual conference and workshop. She has since authored two additional novels, *Meredith's Wolf* and *The Bear at Cinnamon Lake.* All three books are set in the Canadian wilderness, a place that the author revered after unexpectedly falling in love with the area on her first visit. All three books are entertaining and family-friendly with *Meredith's Wolf* written for the Young Adult reading audience (but us older folks find it an equally fun read).

Heartbeats is Judith Barban's second published work of poetry from ThomasMax Publsihing. Her first, released in 2014, was *Crown Jewels.* Among the poems in that book is *Mama,* which was reprinted in this book at the end of the front pages of this book. All of Judith's books are available from Amazon.com, BarnesandNoble.com and most other book sellers, both in print and e-book formats.

www.ingramcontent.com/pod-product-compliance
Lightning Source LLC
Chambersburg PA
CBHW030107070426
42448CB00036B/452
* 9 7 8 1 7 3 7 7 6 2 0 6 5 *